The Earth in space

Nick England

Series editor: Graham Hill

This picture of Jupiter was recorded by the Voyager 1 spacecraft in 1979

Contents

The Orion nebula is a bright cloud of gas and dust where stars are in the process of being born

Activities

Acknowledgements

I would like to thank the following for their help with the production of this book: Dr Peter Hemphill for reading the manuscript and offering advice on astronomy; Graham Hill for advising on the style of the book; Caroline Evans and Lisa Miles of Hodder & Stoughton for their efforts in the later stages of publication.

Nick England
Keswick, January 1991

The publishers would like to thank the following for permission to reproduce their photographs in this book:

Heather Angel (10); Anglo-Australian Telescope Board/Dr David Malin (16 top, bottom; 26 bottom); Armagh Planetarium/NASA (6; 7; 12; 14 bottom right, top left; 15 top right, far left, middle; Genesis Space Photo Library (28 bottom); Hutchinson Picture Library (20); NASA (4; 14 middle left, top middle, top right; 28 top middle, middle left); Royal Observatory, Edinburgh/ Dr David Malin (17 middle); Science Photo Library/Sally Benusen (1982)(14 bottom middle); Science Photo Library/Dr Jeremy Burgess (24 top); Science Photo Library/European Space Agency (18 left; 28 botom right); Science Photo Library/Richard Folwell (18 right); Science Photo Library/T Gull & R Fesen, NASA GSFC (26 top); Science Photo Library/David Hardy (28 top left); Science Photo Library/Denis Milon/Helen & Richard Lines (31 left); Science Photo Library/NASA (1; 5 top; 8 bottom right; 14 bottom left; 15 bottom right; 16 middle; 18 middle; 28 top right, middle bottom); Science Photo Library/ National Optical Astronomy Observatories (17 left); Science Photo Library/ Harvey Pincis (21); Science Photo Library/Ronald Royer (5 bottom); Science Photo Library/John Sandford (8 four left-hand photos; 24 bottom; 31 middle, right).

British Library Cataloguing in Publication Data

England, Nick
The earth in space.
1. Solar system
I. Title II. Series
523.2

ISBN 0 340 53269 6

First published 1991

Typeset by Gecko Ltd, Bicester, Oxon
Printed in Great Britain for the educational publishing division of Hodder and Stoughton Ltd, Mill Road, Dunton Green, Sevenoaks, Kent by Cambus Litho, East Kilbride.

Introduction

Science Scene is a series of books that will help your studies in Key Stage 3 of the National Curriculum.

Each book in the series looks at one of the attainment targets in science. This book – *The Earth in space* – covers the knowledge and understanding in Attainment Target 16 (AT 16 – The Earth in space). As you work through this book you will be able to put the ideas that you read about into practice by doing activities. These will help you to develop some of the skills that are useful in your science studies. The activities will also help you to see how this attainment target overlaps with some of the others that you will meet in Key Stage 3.

There are two parts to the book:

- The first part contains short sections of reading with questions and Things to Do. These sections will help you to understand the important ideas in this topic by reading, thinking and doing. You will read about the Earth and how the solar system works. You will learn about the other planets in the solar system and how we find out about them from Earth. You may already know some of these things. Other facts may be new to you.

- In the second part of the book there are lots of activities. These will give you another chance to learn about the Earth in space, but this time by *doing*. In other words, you will be investigating, thinking and finding out for yourself. Some of the activities are often quite long, and they can be difficult. So, your teacher will help you to choose the activities which are best for you.

If you work through both parts of the book, you will have covered almost all the work that is needed for AT 16 at Key Stage 3. In addition to this your teacher will plan practical work in the laboratory.

We hope that you will enjoy working through *The Earth in space*, and that it will make your science studies exciting and interesting.

Nick England (1991)

The Earth from space

Earth, Moon and Sun

Look at the photograph on the left – it shows the Earth. The photograph was taken from a satellite about 400 000 km above the Earth. Notice that the Earth looks like a large ball floating in space.

The Earth has a diameter of 12 800 km. It is surrounded by a thin layer of air. We need this air to live. The Earth also provides us with food and water. In addition to air, food and water, we also need heat and light. We get these from the Sun. The Sun is a large ball of hot gas, which produces lots of heat and light. The Sun is an example of a **star**. It is our star. The Sun provides the warmth and light to keep the Earth at the right temperature for living things.

Look at the photograph of the Earth again. Which way up do you think it should be? In fact, it does not matter. For us, 'up' is towards the Sky and away from the Earth. 'Down' is towards the Earth. The pull of **gravity** keeps us on the ground. For someone in Australia, 'up' is also towards the sky and 'down' is towards the Earth. The pull of gravity always pulls you towards the Earth and gives you a sense of 'down'.

Day and night

The Earth spins round. It does one full turn in 24 hours. This is why we have days and nights. When our part of the Earth faces the Sun, it is daytime (figure 2). When we cannot see the Sun, it is night. At night we can see lots of stars. These stars are there all the time, but during the day the sky is too bright for us to see them.

Because the Earth is spinning, the Sun and stars seem to move across the sky. Figure 3 shows the path of the Sun across the sky. In the morning, we see it low, in the eastern sky. At midday, it is at its

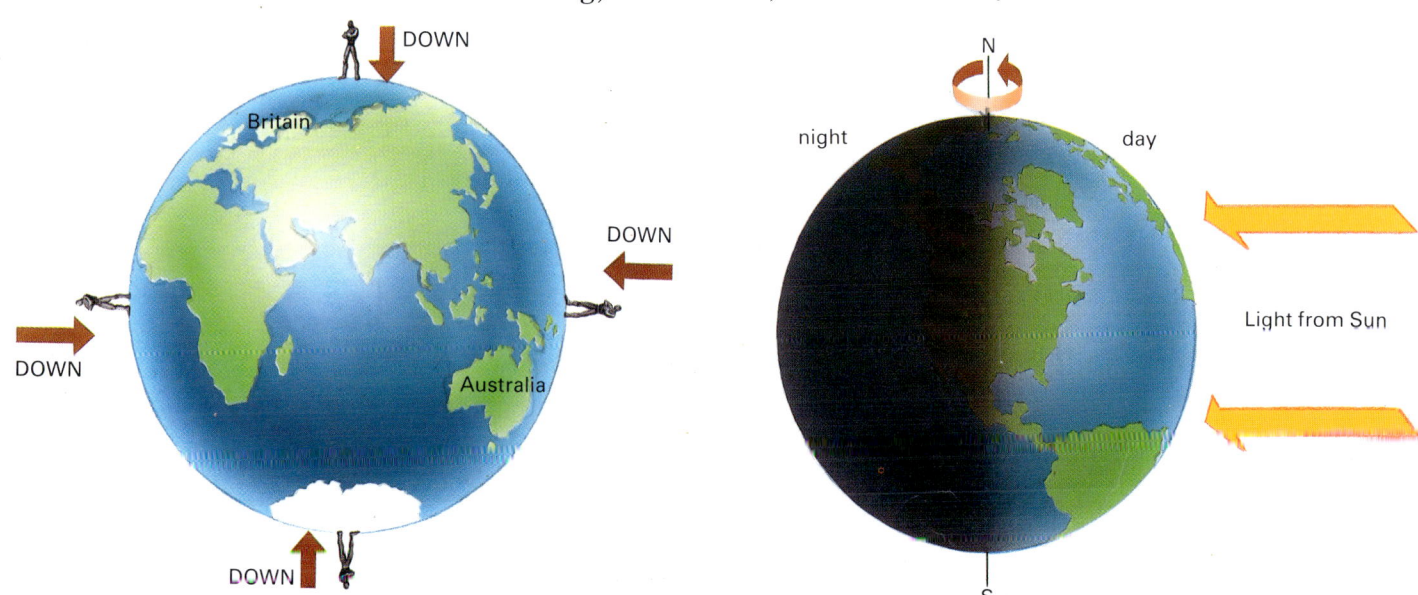

Figure 1 'Down' is always towards the centre of the Earth

Figure 2

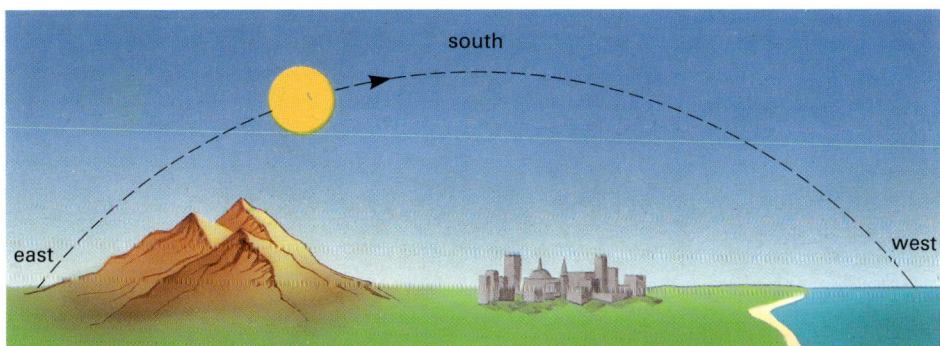

Figure 3 The daily path of the Sun. As the Earth spins, the Sun appears to move across the sky. It rises in the east and sets in the west. At midday, it reaches its highest point

highest point in the sky. In the evening it sets in the west. Now look at figure 4 – you can see that the Sun is seen close to the ground in the morning and evening. At midday the Sun is overhead.

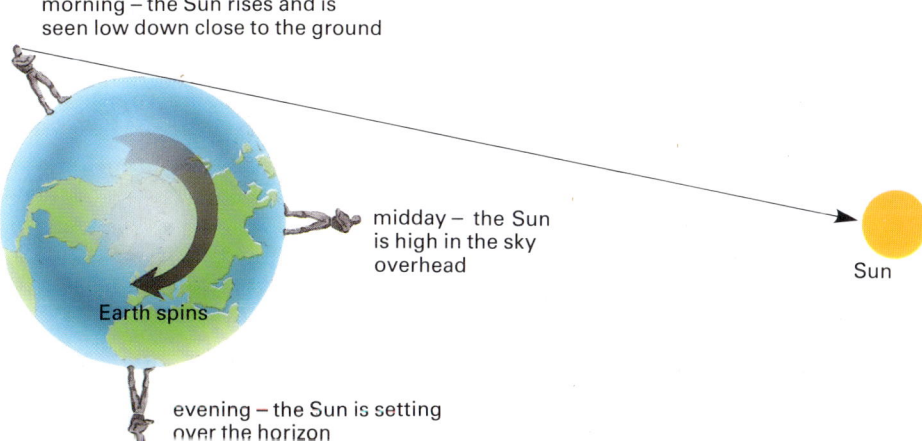

Figure 4

Our most obvious neighbours in space are the Sun and the Moon. The Moon is 400 000 km away from us and has a diameter of 3500 km. The Moon is made from rocks, like the Earth. We see the Moon because it reflects the Sun's light. It does not make its own light

The Sun is 150 million km away from us and has a diameter of 1.4 million km. The Sun makes the light and heat that we need for life

Things to do

1 Draw a diagram to explain why we get days and nights.

2 Imagine that the Earth did not spin.
   a) What would it be like living on Earth?
   b) What would the weather be like?
   c) Where would you like to live?
   d) Would there be day and night?

3 The year is 2030 and you have just become Prime Minister. Get together with some friends and think of the problems that might face you, for example, the world may be facing a population explosion, food shortages, petrol rationing and there may be a hole in the ozone layer above Britain. How might you tackle some of these problems?

4 Copy figure 3. What time of day do you think it is? Mark the time next to the Sun in your diagram. Draw in the position of the Sun at a) midday b) 7 am c) 5 pm.

Figure 1 This diagram shows the relative sizes of the Sun and its planets. The planets are not this close together. Figure 2 shows the positions of the planets better

Mercury's craters

Venus

Jupiter and its moons, Io and Europa

We learnt in Unit 1 that the Earth spins on its axis. In addition to this, the Earth also moves around the Sun. It is called a **planet**. Altogether, there are nine planets that move around the Sun (figure 1). The planets move in curved paths, called **orbits**. The Earth is the third planet out from the Sun. Planets do not shine like the Sun, but we can see them at night because they reflect the Sun's light. The Sun and its nine planets are known as the solar system. The word 'solar' means sun. Some of the planets have other bodies which orbit around them which we call **moons**. The Earth has only one moon. Some planets have several moons.

The four planets closest to the Sun are all rocky with solid surfaces, like the Earth. The planet closest to the sun is Mercury. This has a cratered surface which looks like our Moon's surface. Mercury travels

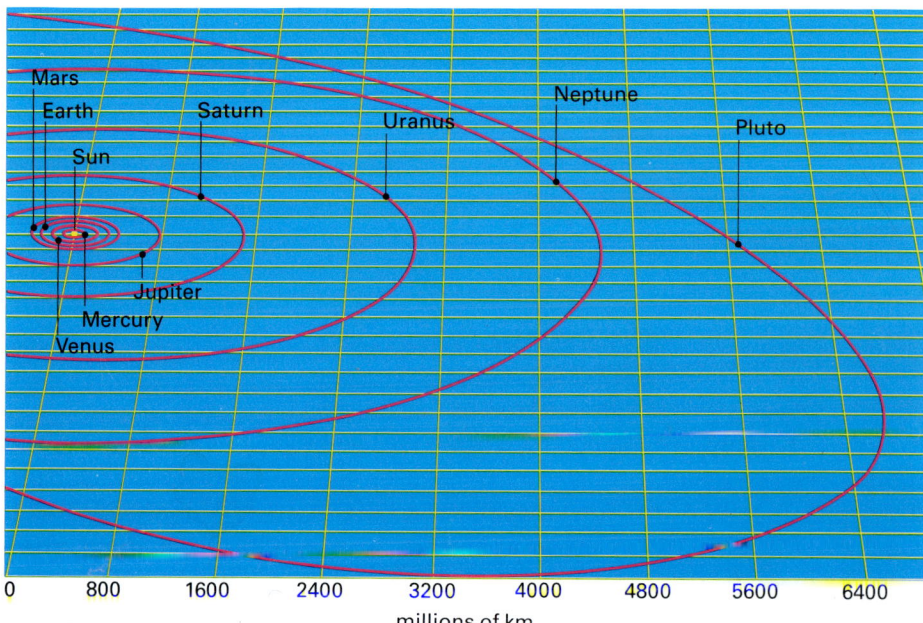

Figure 2 This grid shows the orbits of the planets around the Sun. Notice that the four inner planets are very close to the Sun. The gaps between the outer planets are very large

very quickly around the Sun taking only 88 days to complete one orbit. Venus is nearly the same size as the Earth. It has a dense atmosphere with clouds of sulphuric acid and it is very hot. Nothing could survive on Venus.

Beyond Mars there are 4 giant planets – Jupiter, Saturn, Uranus and Neptune. These planets are made of gas. If you landed on one of them, you would sink into it. The largest planet is Jupiter. This has a diameter eleven times bigger than the Earth. More than 1000 Earths would be needed to fill Jupiter's enormous volume. Jupiter has a giant red spot and fourteen moons. Four of these moons are as big as our own Moon. Saturn is best known for its beautiful rings. The furthest planet from us is Pluto, which is smaller than our Moon. Its temperature is −240°C. From its cold surface, the Sun would only look like a bright star. The Sun could not provide enough light and warmth for us to live on Pluto.

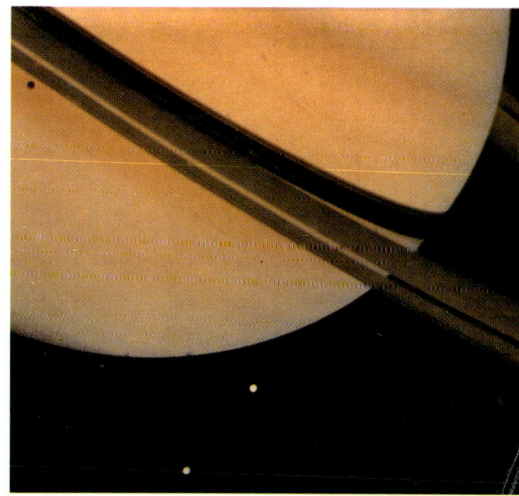

Saturn and its moons and rings

Things to do

1 Use Table 1 to answer these questions.
 a) Which is the smallest planet?
 b) Which is the hottest planet?
 c) Which planet takes just under 2 years to go around the Sun?
 d) How are the temperatures of the planets related to their distance from the Sun?
 e) Is there any pattern in the number of moons planets have? Do big planets have more moons than smaller ones?

2 a) Do you think there could be anything alive on Venus?
 b) Do you think anything could live on Neptune?

3 Get into a group with 2 or 3 others. Make a list of the differences between Saturn and Earth.

Sun facts	
diameter	1 400 000 km
surface temperature	6000°C

Table 1 Information about the planets

Planet	diameter of planet	average distance of planet from Sun	time taken to go round the Sun	number of moons	average temperature on sunny side
Mercury	4900 km	58 million km	88 days	0	350°C
Venus	12 000 km	108 million km	225 days	0	480°C
Earth	12 800 km	150 million km	365¼ days	1	20°C
Mars	6800 km	228 million km	687 days	2	0°C
Jupiter	143 000 km	630 million km	12 years	14	−150°C
Saturn	120 000 km	1430 million km	29 years	18	−190°C
Uranus	52 000 km	2800 million km	84 years	15	−220°C
Neptune	49 000 km	4500 million km	165 years	2*	−240°C
Pluto	3000 km	5900 million km	248 years	1	−240°C

* The photographs from Voyager's flypast in 1989 may reveal more

Our nearest neighbour in space is the Moon. The shape of the Moon always seems to be changing. The position of the Moon in the sky also changes from day to day.

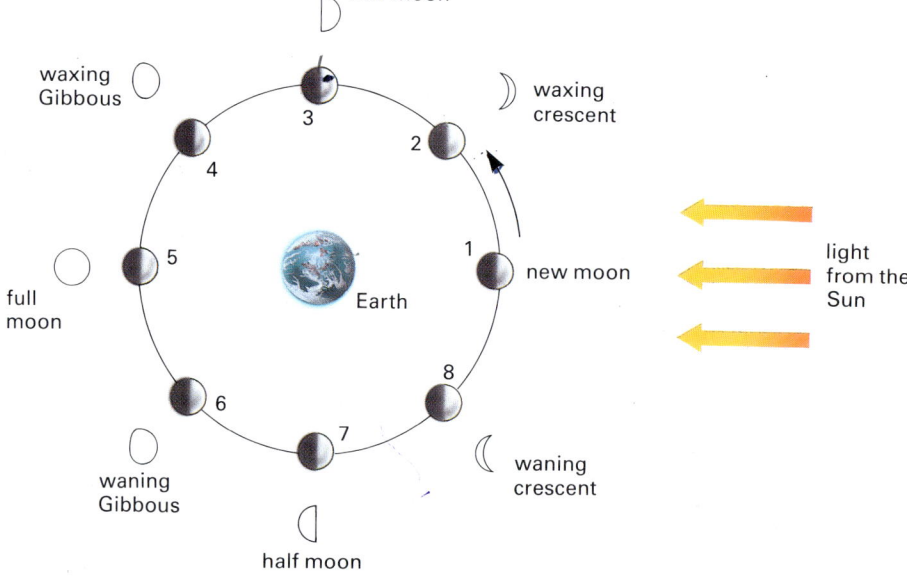

Figure 1 Phases of the Moon

Crescent moon

Gibbous moon

Half moon

The Moon moves around the Earth once a month. This is shown in figure 1. The diagram shows the Moon in eight different places or **phases**. It takes the Moon about $3\frac{1}{2}$ days to move from one position to the next. The Sun shines on the Moon and lights up half of it. In position 1, we cannot see the bright side of the Moon. This is a **new moon** which is very difficult to see. In position 3, we see a **half moon**, since we can see equal amounts of the dark and bright side of the Moon. When the Moon is in position 5, we see all of the bright side of it. This is a **full moon**.

During the first half of the month, the Moon grows from a crescent to a half, to a gibbous and finally, to a full moon. While the Moon is growing, we say it is **waxing**. In the second half of the month, it is **waning**. During this time it shrinks back to a new moon.

Full moon

The Moon was formed 4500 million years ago. At this time its surface was made of molten rock. There were also lots of meteors (rocks) whizzing around in space. The Moon's surface was bombarded by some of these meteors. This caused the cratered surface that we can still see today

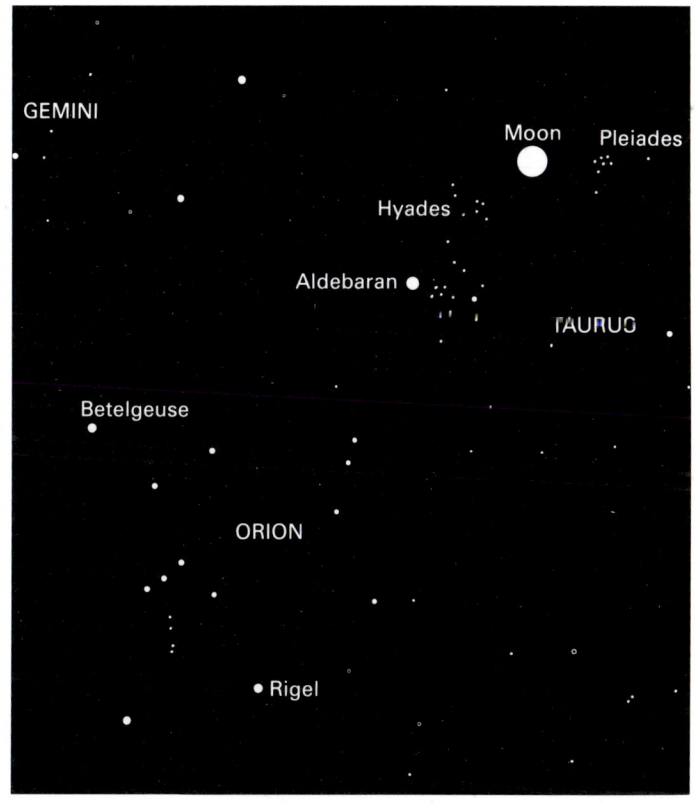

Figure 2 View from Alice's window on December 5th at 11 pm

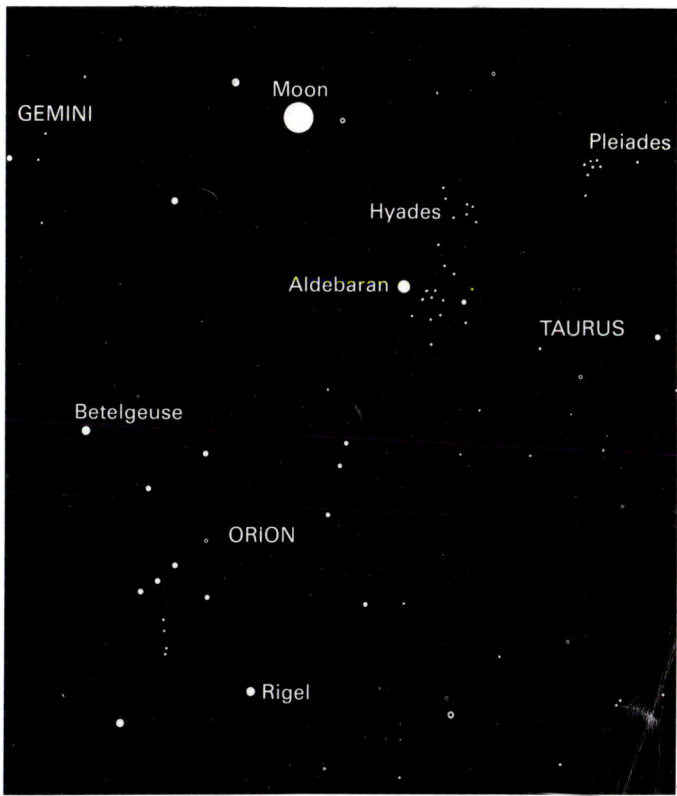

Figure 3 View from Alice's window on December 6th at 11 pm

As the Moon moves round us, we see it close to different stars each night. Figure 2 shows the view south from Alice's bedroom window one night in December. The Moon is near the bright group of stars called the Pleiades. The next night the Moon has moved towards the group of stars called Gemini. Groups of stars are called **constellations**.

Things to do

1 How long does it take the Moon to go once round the Earth?

2 a) Draw a diagram to explain why Alice saw the Moon in different positions each night.

b) Sketch a copy of the stars Alice saw and show where she saw the Moon on December 7th.

c) Look at figure 4. Explain where Alice sees the Moon when she gets up in the morning on December 14th.

3 Get into a group with 2 or 3 others. Make a model to explain the phases of the Moon. You should do this in a darkened room. You will need a bright light and a white football. Try to decide where to put the football to show the different phases.

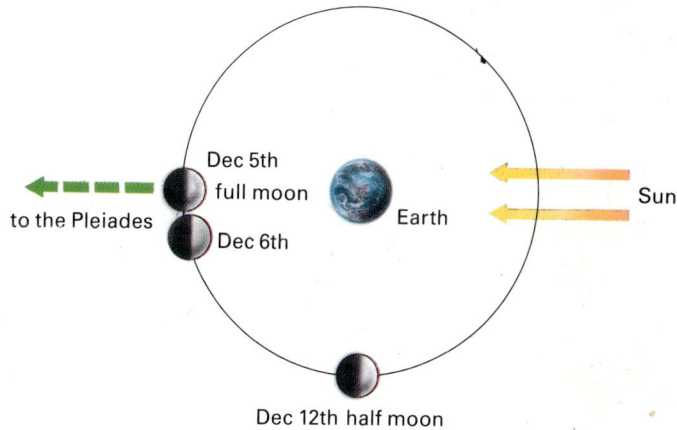

Figure 4 The Moon moves around the Earth, so we see it close to different stars each night

These views show how our landscape changes according to the seasons

The Earth's orbit around the Sun is nearly circular. The closest the Earth gets to the Sun is 147 million kilometres. The furthest the Earth gets from the Sun is 152 million kilometres.

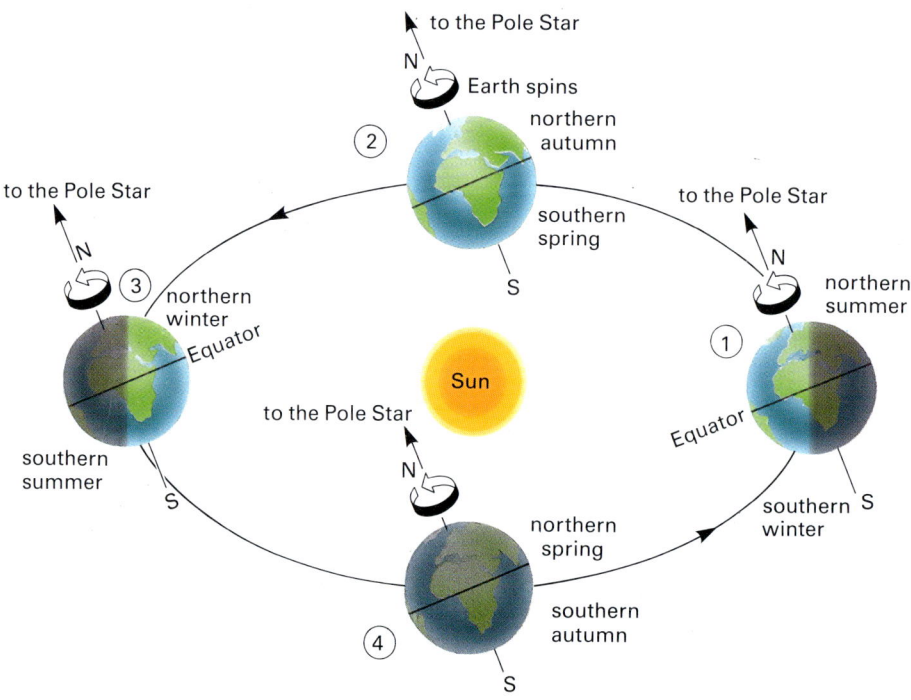

Figure 1 The Earth's path around the Sun

The Earth takes $365\frac{1}{4}$ days to complete its path round the Sun. This is why we have 365 days in our calendar. Every 4 years, we have a leap year with an extra day to make up for the 4 quarters. Look at figure 1 – This shows the Earth's path around the Sun in one year. Remember from Unit 1 that the Earth spins around on an axis. This axis goes through the North and South Poles. This means that the North Pole always points towards the pole star (Polaris). The Earth's axis is also tilted as shown in figure 2. This tilt gives the Earth its seasons.

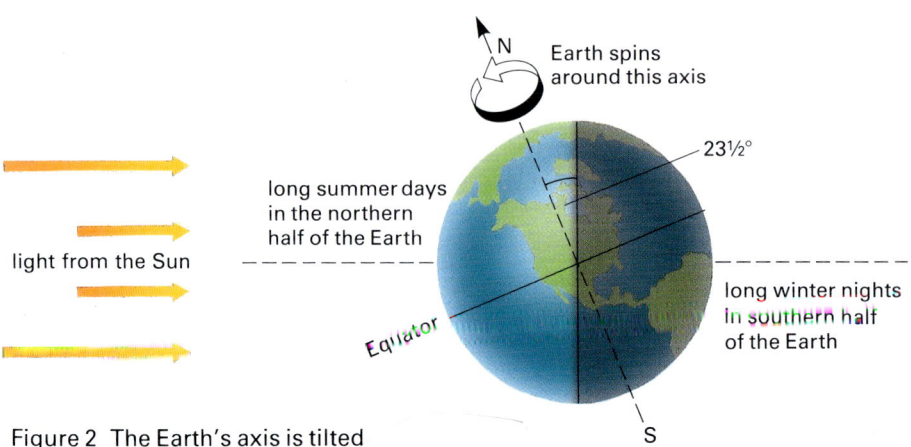

Figure 2 The Earth's axis is tilted

In the middle of our summer, the northern half of the Earth is tipped towards the Sun by an angle of $23\frac{1}{2}°$ (position 1 in figure 1). At this time, the south of the Earth is tipped away from the Sun. Because the north is tipped towards the Sun, it is warmer, which is our summer. But the south is tipped away so there it is colder, and winter. Six months later the Earth has reached position 3 in figure 1. The north is now tipped away from the Sun, and the south is tipped towards the Sun. It is now winter for us and summer in the south. In the spring and autumn, the northern and southern halves of the Earth get equal amounts of sunshine.

The tilt of the Earth's axis also changes the length of our days. In figure 2, you can see that it is summer in the north. Look at the half of the Earth north of the Equator. More of it is in sunlight than in darkness. This means that in summer our days are longer. But look at the part of the Earth south of the Equator. This has more in darkness, so it has long winter nights. During the northern summer, the north pole always sees the Sun. So, it has 24 hours of daylight each day. It never goes dark. But, in the winter, the North Pole has no daylight at all. The Equator has days that are 12 hours long all through the year.

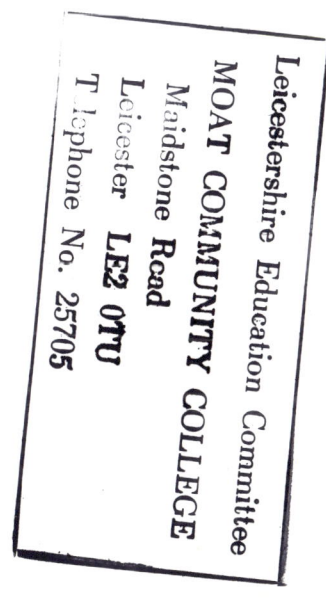
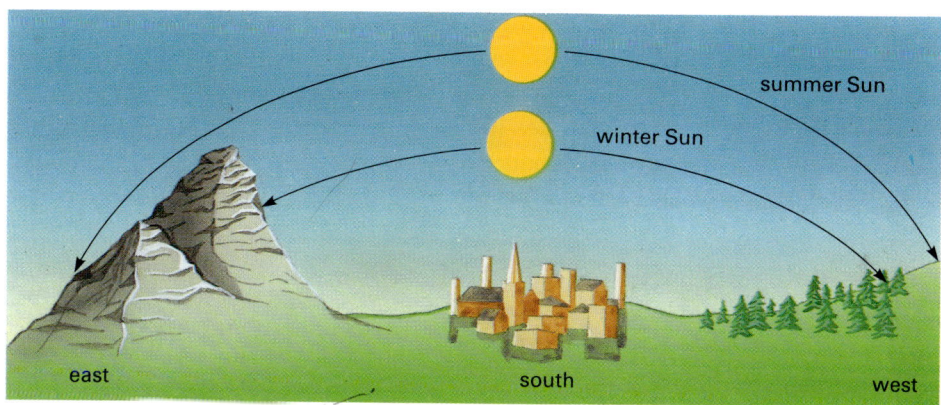

summer Sun

winter Sun

east   south   west

Figure 3 The tilt of the Earth affects the height of the Sun in the sky. In summer we are tipped towards the Sun. This makes it high in the sky. In winter we are tipped away, so the Sun is lower

Things to do

1 Draw a diagram to explain why it is hotter at the Equator than at the North or South Pole.

2 Sita knows it is cold at the North Pole. But she thinks that over a year, someone living at the North Pole would see the Sun for as long as someone living at the Equator. Is she right?

3 Make a model as shown in figure 4 to explain why we get seasons.

match sticks

light bulb

white football

Figure 4

4 Get into a group with 2 or 3 others. Imagine what it would be like on the Earth, if it tilted at different angles.
a) In figure 5a, the Earth does not tilt at all. What happens then? Do we have different seasons? Do the daylight hours change through the year?
b) In figure 5b, the North Pole is facing the Sun. What do you think life will be like now?

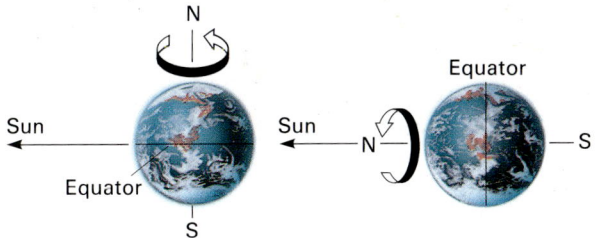

Figure 5a

Figure 5b

5 Moving planets

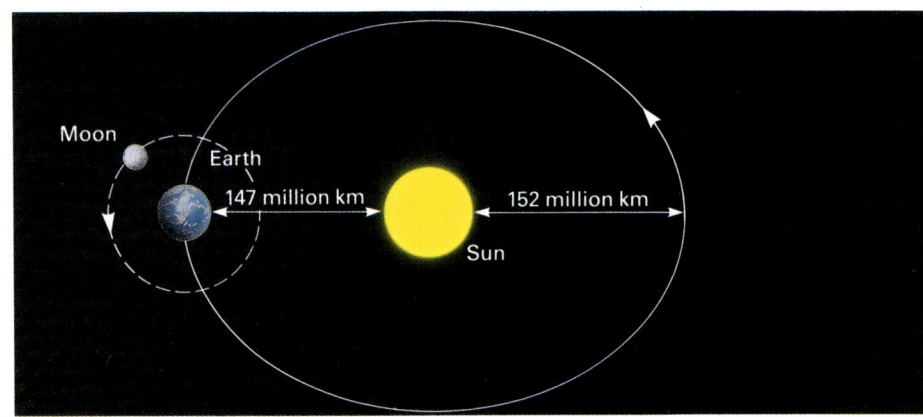

Figure 1 The Earth moves in an elliptical orbit round the Sun. The Moon moves around the Earth

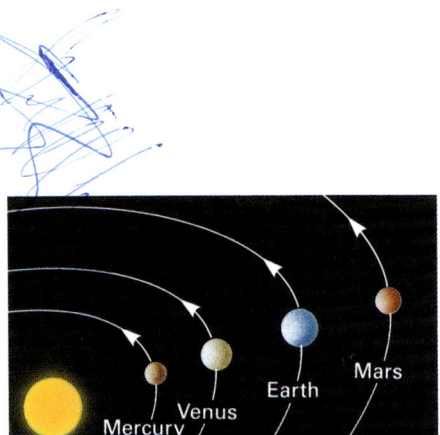

Figure 2 All planets rotate around the Sun in the same direction

Figure 3 All planets lie very close to the same plane. Will all planets always be on the same side of the Sun?

Saturn does not stay still. It moves round the Sun and we see it move past the stars. As it moves round the Sun, we see its rings at different angles

The Earth moves round the Sun in a curved path. The shape of this path is an **ellipse**. An ellipse is a bit like a squashed circle. Look at figure 1. This shows how the Moon moves round the Earth and how the Earth moves round the Sun. All the planets move in elliptical paths round the Sun. They all move in the same direction, which you can see in figure 2. The planets near the Sun move faster than those further away. Look at figure 2 and imagine that you are looking down on the solar system from above. Now suppose you could look at the solar system from the side (figure 3). In this case, you would be able to see all the planets in nearly the same plane. This plane is called the **plane of the ecliptic**. Our Moon also lies in the same plane. This means that quite often you can see the Moon close to some planets in the sky. If you see a bright 'star' close to the Moon it is probably a planet.

In ancient Greece, the word 'planet' meant 'wanderer'. The planets were given this name because they appear to wander around the sky. You will remember from the last unit that the Earth moves round the Sun once a year. In July we are always in the same position in relation to the Sun. So, we see the same stars at night each year in July. The stars are so far away that they do not appear to move at all, even over thousands of years. Each July, we see the bright star, Antares, low in the sky. From 1984 to 1988 Saturn could also be seen clearly on July

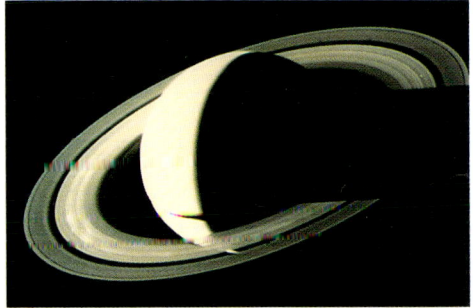

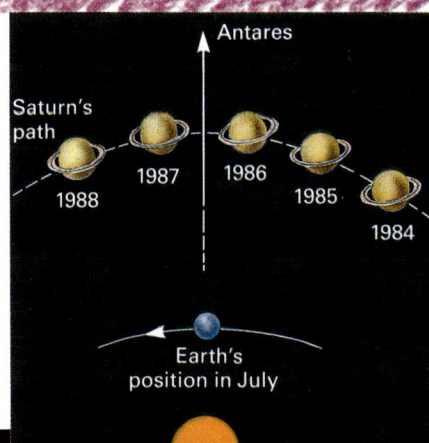

evenings. But Saturn moves slowly round the Sun, taking about 30 years to go once round. During 1986 and 1987 Saturn moved slowly past Antares. This is shown in figure 4. Saturn will be close to Antares again in the year 2016.

Figure 4 As Saturn moves slowly round the Sun, we see it move against the stars

Things to do

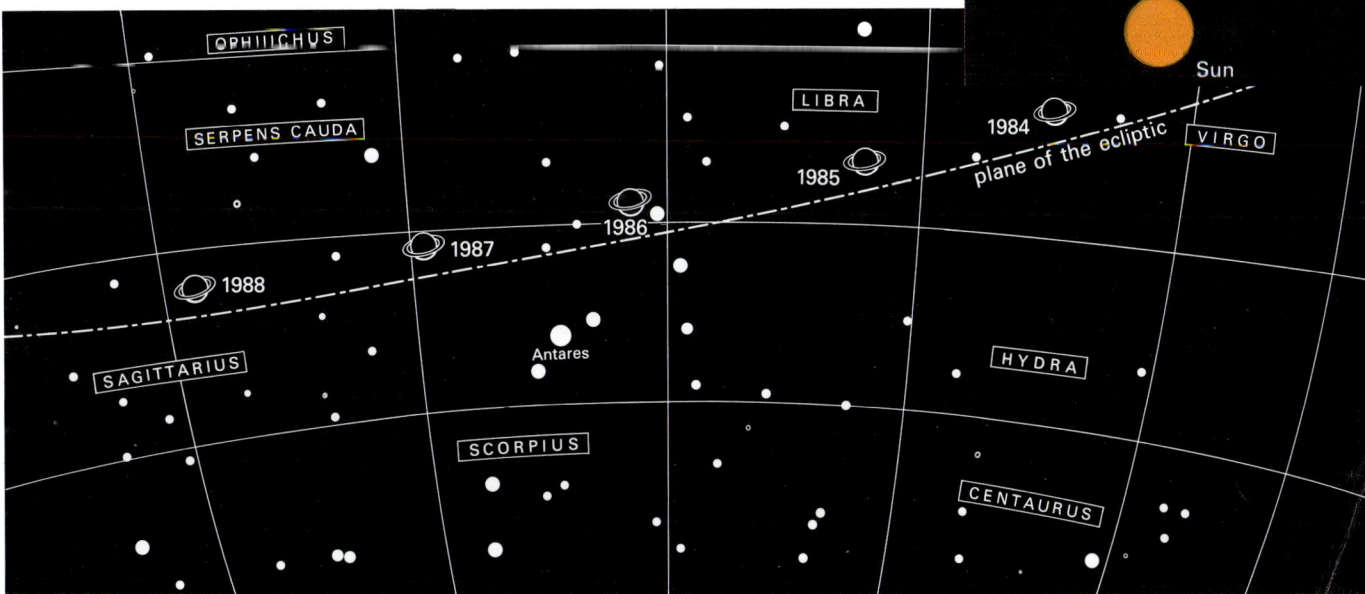

Figure 5 This shows how Saturn moved past the stars over a period of 5 years. Note that the planet always lies close to the plane of the ecliptic

1 Look at the star map in figure 5, approximately where will you see Saturn in 2014? (*Hint*: How long does Saturn take to go once round the sun?)

2 If you look at Jupiter or Saturn through a telescope you will see a large planet with markings on it. If you look at Pluto through a telescope, it looks like a dull star.

a) Why do you think Pluto looks so dull?

b) Pluto was not discovered until 1930. How did astronomers know it was a planet and *not* a fixed star?

3 In this activity you will be drawing ellipses. Work in pairs. Make a loop using 30 cm of cotton thread. Fix a sheet of white paper onto a drawing board. Put two drawing pins about 6 cm apart near the centre of the paper (figure 6). Pull the cotton tight with a pencil. Now, move the pencil round the curve as shown in the figure.

The Earth follows an elliptical path like this. Where should the Sun be placed on this model? Make another

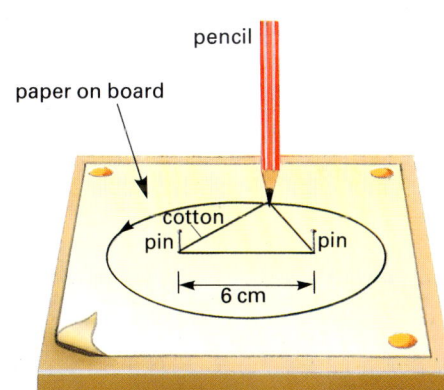

Figure 6

ellipse, but this time have the pins 12 cm apart. How does the shape of the ellipse change as the pins are moved further apart?

4 In contrast to Saturn, Mars is much closer to the Earth and much closer to the Sun.

a) Why does Mars appear as a brighter planet than Saturn?

b) Why does Mars seem to move across the star pattern more quickly than Saturn?

6   Exploration of space

Thousands of years ago, our ancestors marvelled at the stars and planets. They looked at them at night and wondered what they were. The ancient Greeks developed their mathematical skills to work out the positions and movements of the stars and planets.

In the last forty years, we have used modern technology to explore our solar system. People have travelled far away into space. The first satellite was put into orbit around the Earth in 1957. The first person to orbit the Earth in a satellite was Yuri Gagarin. The same year, President Kennedy announced that the Americans would land a person on the Moon. This aim was achieved on July 20th 1969. On that day, Neil Armstrong stepped on to the Moon's surface.

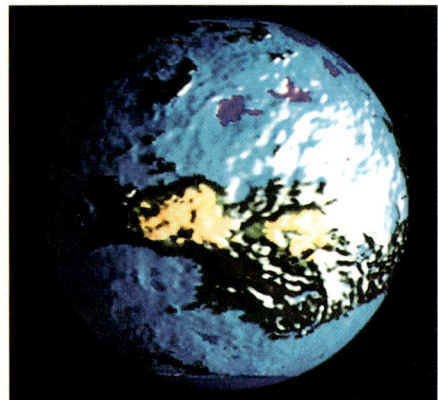

This radar map shows up the mountains on Venus

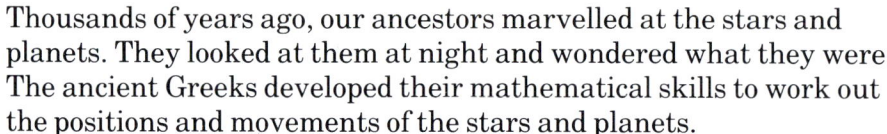

Rills (trenches) and mountains on the Moon

Astronaut Edwin E Aldrin – he and Neil Armstrong were the first men to stand on the Moon

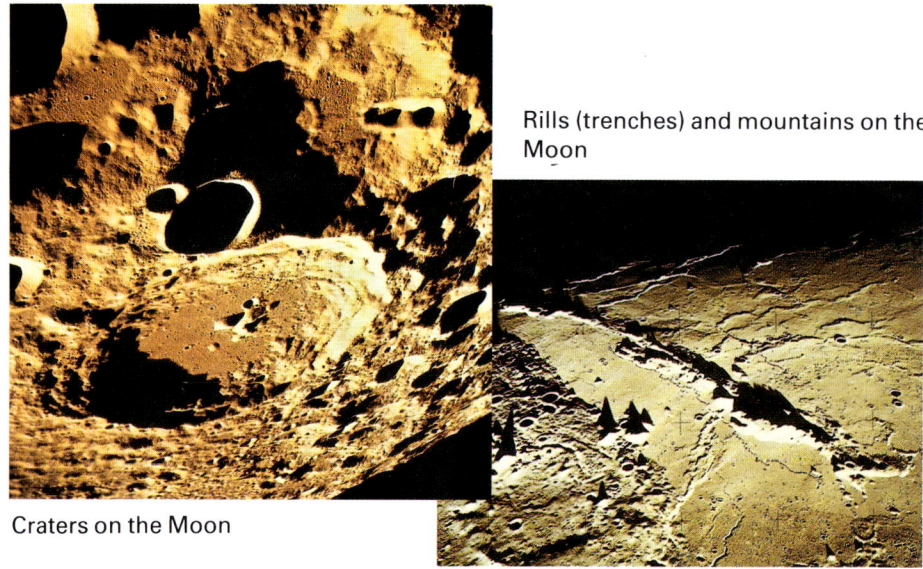

Craters on the Moon

In the last 20 years, about 40 unmanned space probes have explored the solar system. The only planet that has not been visited is Pluto. In the 1970s the Americans launched a series of *Mariner* probes. The first ones explored Mercury, Venus and Mars. The later ones explored Jupiter and Saturn. In 1976, *Viking 1* landed on Mars and sent back pictures of a red, dusty and rocky surface.

The surface of Mars

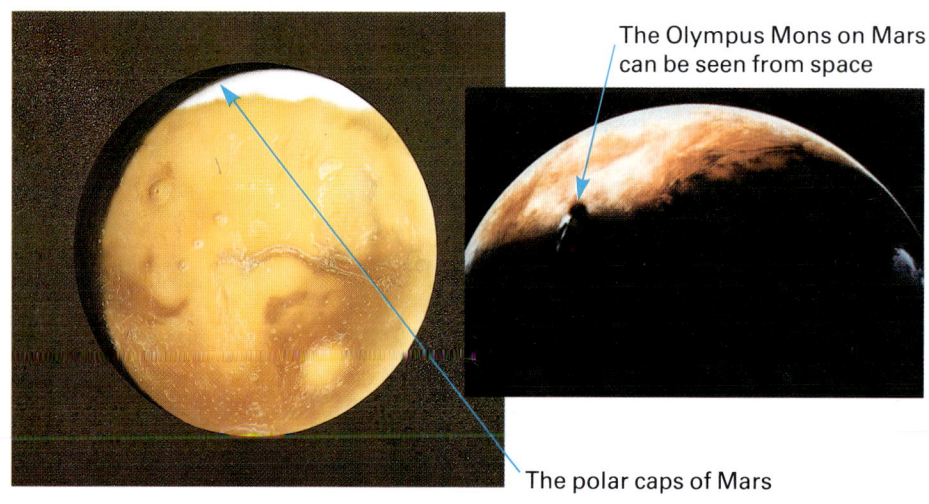

The Olympus Mons on Mars can be seen from space

The polar caps of Mars

The most successful and exciting probes of all were *Voyager 1* and *Voyager 2*. These probes were launched in 1977. *Voyager 1* visited Jupiter and Saturn. *Voyager 2* went on to Uranus in 1986 and Neptune in 1989.

The photographs that were sent back amazed the world. The swirling clouds of Jupiter blow around with hurricane wind speeds of 200 miles (320 km) per hour. The weather patterns are caused by the rapid rotation of this giant planet. Jupiter takes only 10 hours to rotate once. Io, one of Jupiter's moons, has many active volcanoes.

The highlight of the *Voyager* mission was the encounter with Saturn. Photographs showed thousands of rings held in position by small moons. The rings are made of dust and millions of rocks.

In the next section we turn to the stars. This is a world of super giants and dwarfs, supernovas and black holes.

Jupiter

Jupiter with its moon Io

Saturn's rings

Mimas – one of Saturn's moons

Things to do

1 Try to answer the following questions about the solar system. You may need to go to the library to find some books to help you.

a) Which planet has a red spot and some white ovals in its clouds?

b) Which is the red planet?

c) How many planets have rings round them?

d) Jupiter has 4 large moons. What are they called? Who discovered them?

e) Which planets show phases, like the Moon?

f) Which planets have ice caps at their north and south poles?

g) Where would you find Oberon and Titania?

h) What are asteroids?

i) Which planet has the most moons?

j) Which planet has the shortest day?

k) Where would you find the sea of tranquility?

l) Where is Olympus Mons?

2 Imagine that you are Neil Armstrong stepping onto the Moon on 20th July, 1969. Describe how you felt. Write down what you would say at your first press interview on return to Earth.

There are more stars in the sky than there are grains of sand on the beach. Here you can see stars in the Milky Way

The Andromeda galaxy is a spiral galaxy like ours. It contains over 100000 million stars. Light would take 150000 years to cross it. Notice that Andromeda has two neighbouring dwarf galaxies

A spiral galaxy

Figure 1 a) a side view of our galaxy b) a top view of our galaxy. If you look towards the centre of our galaxy you see part of the Milky Way. On dark summer nights, this looks like a milky band overhead, but it is made from billions of stars

Look at the sky on a dark clear night. How many stars do you think you can see? All of these stars are great distances away from us. We measure the distances to stars in **light years**. A light year is the distance that light travels in one year. This is about 10 million million km. The brightest star in the sky is Sirius. It is also one of the nearest, but light takes 9 years to reach us from Sirius. Light only takes 6 hours to reach Pluto from the Sun. This makes our solar system look very small.

Try to look at the sky on a clear night through binoculars or a telescope. You will be able to see even more stars. Look at the photograph of the Milky Way opposite. Many of the stars in the Milky Way have their own solar systems. Perhaps there are planets like Earth.

Clusters of millions of stars like the Milky Way are called **galaxies**. The Sun is one of the stars in the Milky Way (figure 1). The Milky Way has about 100000 million stars in it. If you could see our galaxy from the side, it would look like two fried eggs stuck back to back (figure 1). It is long and thin except for a bulge in the middle. If you could see the galaxy from the top it would look like a giant whirlpool with great spiral arms. The galaxy spins round. Our Sun takes about 220 million years to go round the centre of the galaxy. In millions of years time, people will see different stars at night.

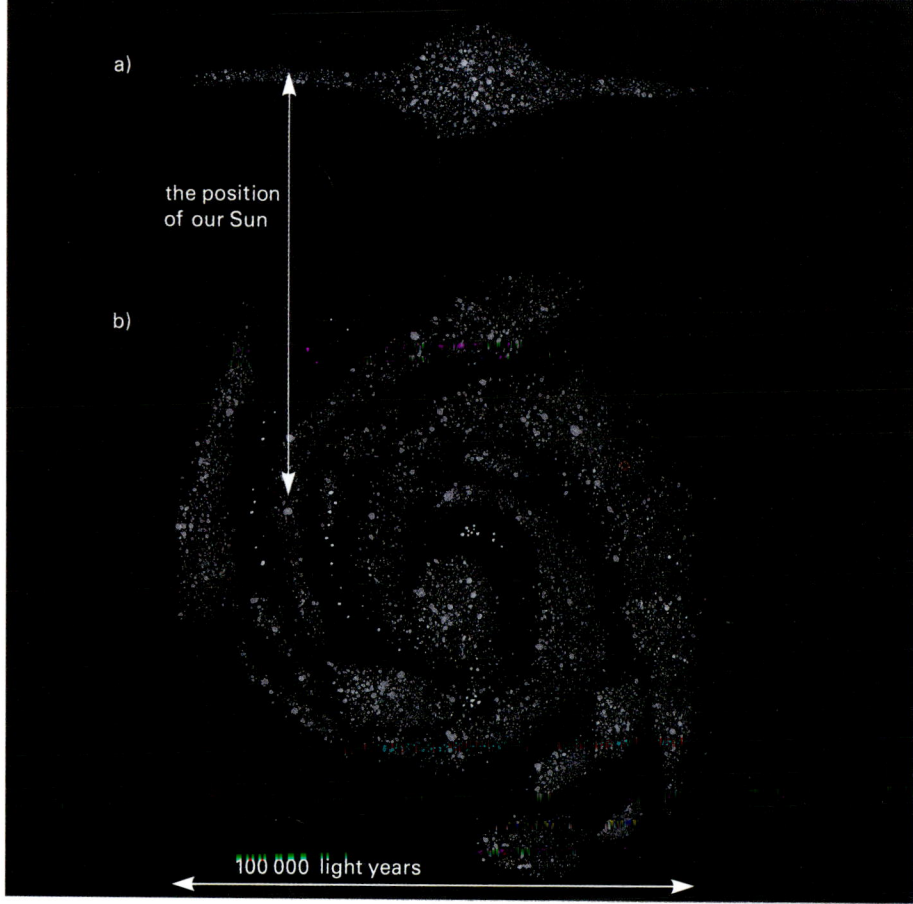

a)

the position of our Sun

b)

100 000 light years

Our Sun is quite small for a star. It is called a yellow dwarf, see figure 2. Betelgeuse is one of the brightest and largest stars in the constellation of Orion. Its diameter is over 500 times larger than our Sun's diameter. Rigel is even brighter than Betelgeuse. Rigel is called a blue giant. It shines more brightly than 10 000 Suns. If you turn back to Unit 3 you can see the position of these two giants.

Our galaxy is not alone in space. The Milky Way is one of millions of galaxies. One of the nearest to us that you can see from Britain is the Andromeda Galaxy. This is 2 million light years away. The most distant galaxies in the universe are 15 000 million light years away from us. When light left them, the Earth did not exist!

The bright star Sandulek 89 turned into a supernova in 1987. A supernova is the most dramatic of cosmic events. For a week, the star outshone the whole of the Magalan Cloud, which is Sandulek's galaxy. A large star at the end of its life collapses and then explodes – this is a supernova

Betelgeuse – a red supergiant (500 Sun diameters)

Rigel – a blue giant (10 Sun diameters)

Sun – a yellow dwarf

Sirius B – a white dwarf (0.03 Sun diameters)

▲ Here you can see the true scale of the universe. Each one of these blurred objects is a galaxy as large as our own

Figure 2 Stars come in all sizes

Things to do

1 Put in order of size starting with the largest:

red giant, galaxy, planet, yellow dwarf, universe.

2 Use your own words to explain what we mean by

- galaxy
- constellation
- star
- planet.

3 In the universe there are over 10 billion galaxies. Each galaxy has about 100 billion stars in it. (1 billion = 1000 million.)
  a) Work out how many stars there are in the universe.

b) Do you think it is possible there may be life somewhere else other than Earth?

4 Look at the table of information about stars. These stars are like our Sun.
  a) Is there a connection between the brightness of a star and its temperature?
  b) Is there a connection between the brightness of a star and its diameter?

Table 1 Information about stars

Star	Temperature of surface in °C	Diameter relative to our Sun	Mass relative to our Sun	Brightness relative to our Sun
β Centauri	19 000	6	4	4000
Vega	10 600	2.6	3	100
Altair	8200	1.9	2	15
Sun	5800	1	1	1
61 Cygni A	3900	0.7	0.5	0.1

It is obvious to us that the Earth is a sphere. After all, satellites go round the Earth every day. They send back photographs of a curved surface. The first astronauts who went to the Moon looked back and saw it was a big ball. But, people have not always thought the Earth was a sphere. In 600 BC, the Greeks thought the Earth was flat. They believed that they lived on a flat Earth, which was surrounded by sea (figure 1). They thought that the Earth was at the centre of everything. The stars, Sun and Moon went round us each day. People thought that you could fall off the 'underneath' of a sphere. They had no idea about gravity. So they could not understand how gravity would always pull you towards the Earth.

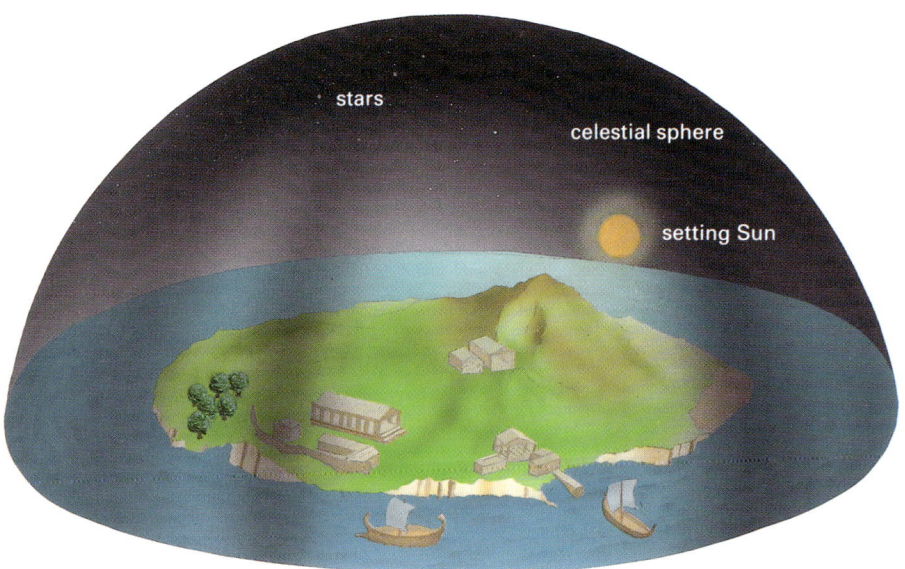

Figure 1 Flat Earth

However, careful observations and measurements soon showed the Greeks that the Earth was really a sphere.

They watched ships slowly disappear below the horizon. At sea, they knew what it was like to be surrounded by a circular horizon. This suggested that the surface of the Earth was probably curved.

From space wo can tell what the weather is like on Earth

Modern photographs from space show us that the Earth is a sphere

Objects on the horizon disappear as we move away from them. This show us that the Earth is not flat

They also noticed that as you go further north, the Pole Star appears higher in the sky at night and the Sun lower at day. In 330 BC, Eratosthenes used this idea to measure the radius of the Earth. Eratosthenes lived in Alexandria which was 800 kilometres north of Syene, now Aswan in Egypt. He knew that in midsummer each year the Sun was directly overhead at noon in Syene. This was because sunbeams falling into a deep well were reflected back up again by the water at the bottom (figure 2a). At noon on midsummer's day, he measured the shadow of a tall obelisk in Alexandria. He found that the sunbeams made an angle of 8° with the vertical (figure 2b). This showed Eratosthenes that the Earth had a curved surface. It also allowed him to work out the Earth's radius. This is something you can do in question 4 below.

Figure 2 a) At noon in Syene, the Sun is overhead b) Midsummer noon in Alexandria c) The Sun is not overhead in Alexandria because the Earth is a sphere

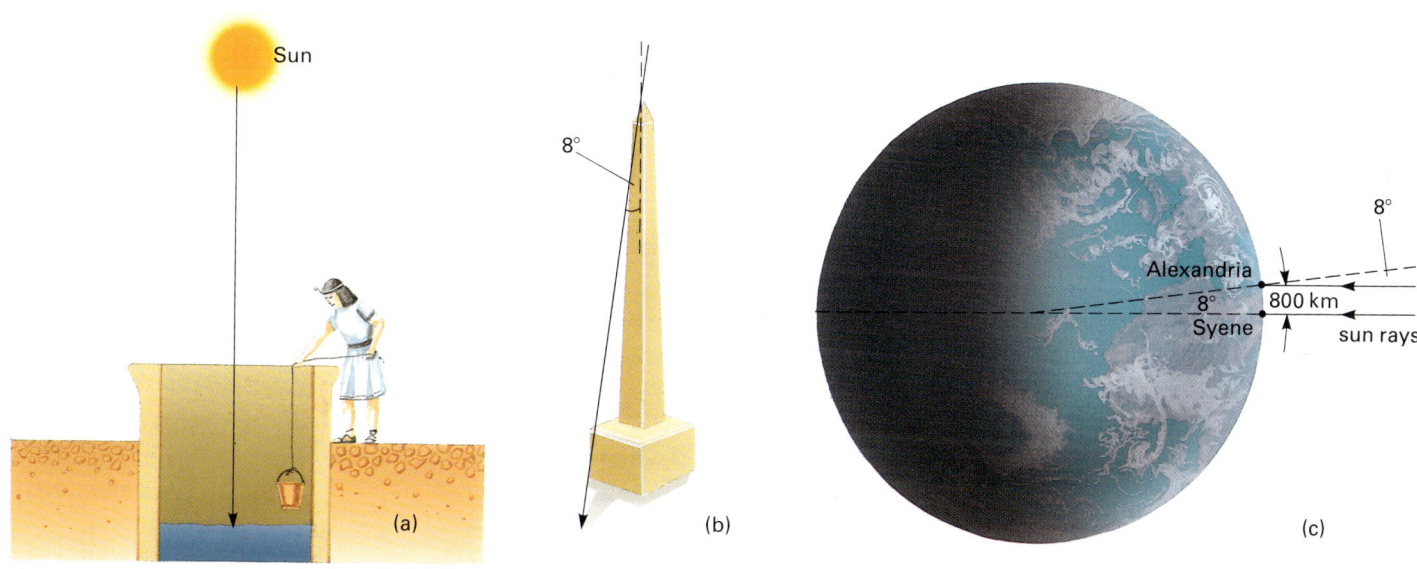

Things to do

1 In 1492 Christopher Columbus sailed from Europe and encountered America.

  a) At the time, some people worried that he might fall off the edge of the Earth. Why were they worried?

  b) Suppose you are Christopher Columbus. What would you say to your sailors to persuade them that they would not fall off the edge of the world during the voyage?

2 Draw a diagram to explain why ships disappear over the horizon at sea.

3 At the North Pole, the Pole Star appears overhead. At the Equator, the Pole Star appears close to the northern horizon.

  a) Why does this show the Earth is curved? Explain by drawing a diagram.

  b) What would the directions of the Pole Star be if the Earth was flat?

4 This question is about Eratosthenes's measurements.

  a) Eratosthenes measured the distance from Syene to Alexandria. How do you think he did it?

  b) Explain why Eratosthenes took more than a year to make his observations. (*Hint*: He could not travel very quickly in those days!)

  c) Look at figure 2c. Explain why you cover a distance of 100 km if you go 1° north from Syene.

  d) There are 360° in a circle. What distance do you go if you walk right round the Earth?

  e) This distance is about 6 times the radius of the Earth. Calculate the Earth's radius.

Activities

1 Following the Sun

In this activity you will be finding out where the Sun rises and sets. But, take great care while doing this. **NEVER LOOK DIRECTLY AT THE SUN**. This will hurt your eyes and will probably damage them.

Use a compass to find out where south is. Then find a place where you can look south. This could be from an upstairs window or from the road or garden. Use your compass to find the direction of the sun at:

■ 9.00 am   ■ 1.00 pm

■ 12.00 noon   ■ 4.00 pm

1 At what time was the Sun due south?
2 At what time was the Sun highest in the sky?
3 Make sketches to show the path of the Sun as it crosses the sky. You may need more than one diagram.

At what part of the day do you think this photo was taken?

2 A model solar system

In this activity, the class will be forming a model of our solar system. Your teacher will divide the class into 10 groups. One group will act as the Sun. Each of the other groups will act as one of the planets. The scale of our solar system will be 1 m for 10 million km.*

1 Each planet group must calculate how far they must place themselves from the Sun. You will need to look at table 1 on page 7.
2 When you have finished your claculation, your teacher will take you outside to form the model in the school grounds. Each planet must pace out its distance from the Sun. This model should give you an idea of the size of the solar system. Notice that the far planets are a lot further away from the Sun than the Earth.
3 When you get back to the classroom, work out where the nearest star (Alpha Centauri) would be on this model. Would it be in the next street, the next town, or the next county perhaps? (Alpha Centauri is 6000 times further away from the Sun than Pluto.)

(*This may be too big a scale. You may need to choose 1 m for 20 million km).

3 Moon shapes

Find out from the newspaper or a diary when the next new moon is. Two days later look for the Moon, just after the Sun has set. Draw carefully the shape of the Moon which is now 2 days old. Draw the shape for as many days as you can during the month. (When the Moon is full you may have to stay up late to see it.) When the Moon is waning, you will have to get up early in the morning.

Record your shapes carefully using a table similar to Table 1 opposite.

If you have a pair of binoculars, try to draw the surface shading on the Moon. You should be able to work in some 'seas' and 'craters'. 'Seas' are large plains on the Moon.

Date	Age of Moon	Shape
March 2	0	
March 5	3 days	🌙

4 Following the Moon

If the weather is clear, you can do this activity at the same time as Activity 3.

1 Each day, when you draw the Moon during the month, make a sketch to show the stars near to it.

2 Draw a new sketch each day to show how the Moon moves past the stars.
3 If possible, label the brightest stars on your sketches.

5 Making a sundial

Figure 1

On a bright sunny day, get up early and stick a peg or a pole straight up in the ground. Each hour put a small peg into the ground to mark the end of the shadow. Then put numbers next to the shadow to mark the time.

Then, the next day, get a friend to see if he or she can read the time without a clock.

1 When was the shadow the shortest?
2 Did it agree with noon of your watch?
3 During 'summer time' the Sun is at its highest at 1 pm and *not* 12 noon. Why is this?

What time is it?

21

6 Measuring the Sun's inclination

Use the same pole or peg as you used for your sundial in Activity 5.

1 Measure the height of the pole or peg above the ground.
2 At midday, measure the length of its shadow.
3 Make a scale drawing of your results similar to figure 1 opposite.
4 Measure the angle θ with a protractor. This is called the Sun's inclination.
5 Repeat the experiment and measure the angle again in a month's time at midday. Is the angle larger or smaller? Is the angle larger in summer or winter?

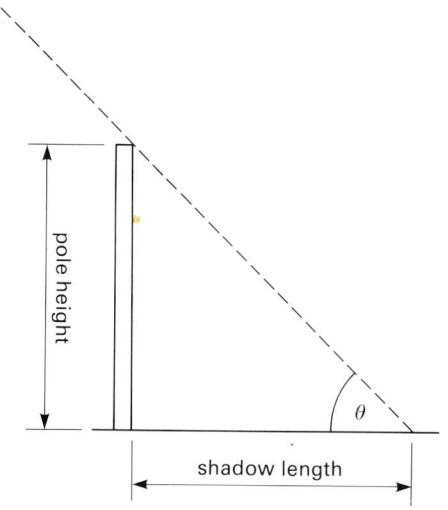

Figure 1

7 Phases of the Moon

Get into a small group with 2 or 3 others. Paint one half of a large ball black and paint the other half white. You can now use this to demonstrate the phases of the Moon (see figure 2 below). Most of your group should stand still while one person walks around them, always keeping the white side of the ball pointing in the same direction.

1 Draw what you see.
2 Why must the white side of the ball always point in the same direction?

group
stands
here

pupil rotates

Figure 2

8 Planet motion

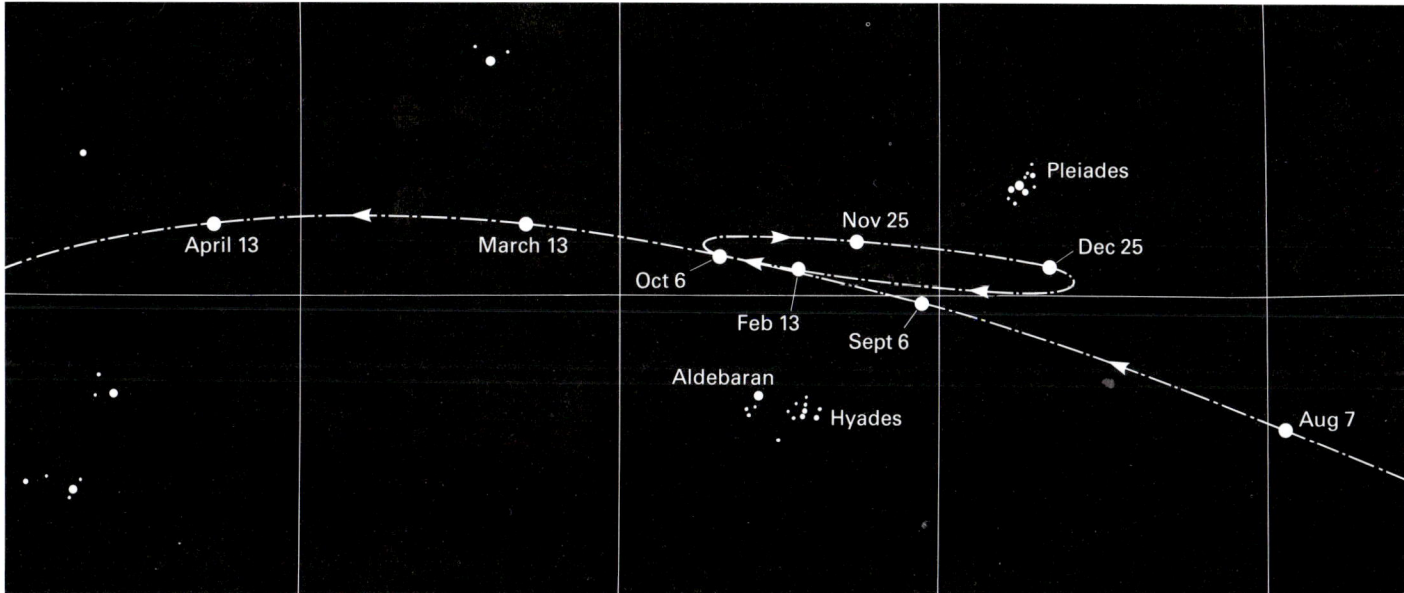

Figure 3

The star chart below shows how Mars moved past the **Pleiades** and **Hyades** in late 1990 and early 1991. In November, December and January, Mars appeared to go through a backwards loop. This was because the Earth overtook Mars in their movements around the Sun. When you overtake something it seems to go backwards.

1 Make a rough sketch of the path Mars followed.
2 Where do you think Mars was on   (i) July 7th 1990   (ii) April 1st 1991?
3 Can you find Mars, Jupiter or Saturn in the night sky? Watch the motion of the planets over the next few months. Look in *The Times* newspaper at the end of the month for a star map to help you.

9 Explaining planet motion

This activity will help you to understand how Mars or Jupiter move against the background stars.

1 First you need to position some 'stars'. These can be trees or posts or even pupils placed about 100 m from the rest of the class.
2 One person acts as Mars. He or she should be about 30 m from the class and walk slowly as shown in the diagram.
3 The rest of the class walk quickly round in a circle, watching Mars.
4 Describe how Mars appears to move against the background stars.
5 Every 'year' Mars appears to go backwards for two

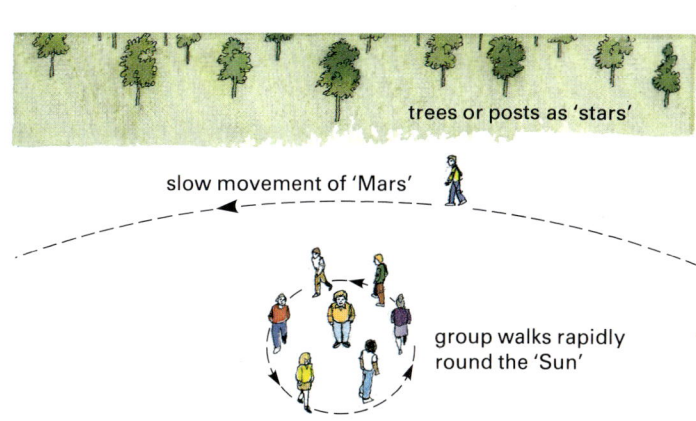

trees or posts as 'stars'

slow movement of 'Mars'

group walks rapidly round the 'Sun'

Figure 4

or three months, before continuing forwards. Try to explain this motion.

10 Galileo and Copernicus

During the 16th century, both Galileo and Copernicus got into serious trouble with the Catholic Church. Their scientific beliefs did not agree with the views of the Church. In the 16th century the Church preached that the Earth was the centre of the universe. After all, the church believed that God had created the Earth and had made humans in his own image. We were thought to be the most important things in God's creation. So, it seemed reasonable to the Church that we were at the centre of things. The Church also preached that the Earth was a perfect sphere. And so were the planets, the Sun and the Moon. Everything rotated around the Earth.

Nicholas Copernicus was the first to challenge the church's teaching. He said that the Sun was the centre of our solar system. All planets went round it, including the Earth. He also said that the Earth turned on its axis every day and that the stars did not go around us. This is what we believe today. Copernicus could explain the motion of the planets easily with the Sun at the centre of the solar system. It was very difficult to explain the motion of the planets with the Earth at the centre.

In 1610, Galileo heard about the invention of a telescope. He made one for himself and used it to look at the Moon, Venus, Jupiter, Saturn and Mars. He also used it to project an image of the Sun onto a screen.

Galileo discovered that the Moon had craters, the Sun had spots and Saturn had 'ears'. He found that Venus had phases like our Moon, Mars varied in brightness and that Jupiter had some moons of its own. Several of Galileo's observations supported the ideas of Copernicus.

Copernicus

A modern astronomer's telescope

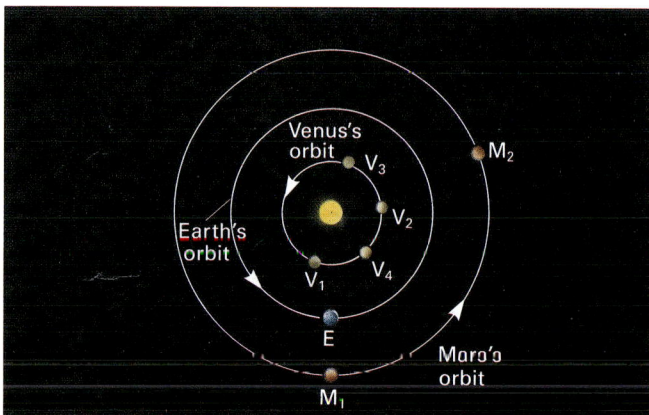
Figure 1

1 What do you think Saturn's 'ears' were?

2 Why do you think that the Church was unhappy to hear that the Sun had spots and that the Moon had craters?

3 Figure 1 shows how Copernicus and Galileo thought the planets moved. Will Mars appear brighter in position M_1 or M_2? Explain your choice.

4 Figure 2 shows four different phases of Venus seen through Galileo's telescope

   (i)   Which phase corresponds to each of the positions V_1, V_2, V_3 and V_4?

   (ii) Explain why these phases happen.

   (iii) Why does Venus seem to change in size?

5 The series of diagrams in figure 3 show what Galileo saw on five nights when he looked at Jupiter.

   (i)   What are the dots?

   (ii) Why did the dots move?

   (iii) Why did he see 4 dots on some nights and only 3 dots on other nights?

   (iv) Why did this discovery make it seem more reasonable for the planets to move round the Sun?

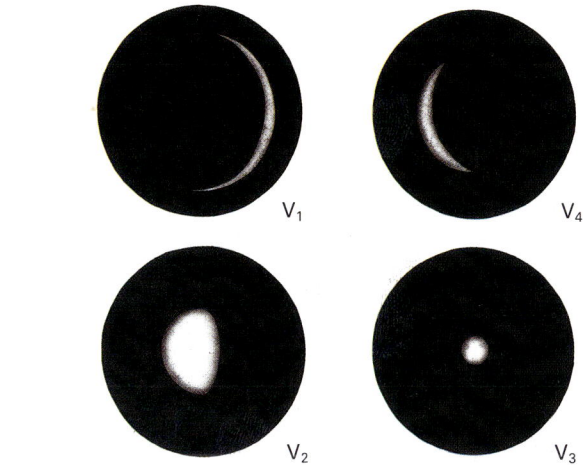

Figure 2

night 1

night 2

night 3

night 4

night 5

Figure 3

11   Ursa Major and Casseopeia

In this activity you are going to find two well known constellations, Ursa Major and Casseopeia. Both of these constellations are close to the Pole Star. They can be seen all year round. Ursa Major (figure 4) is also known as the Great Bear, or the Plough.

The two stars on the right of the Plough are known as the pointers. These point towards the Pole Star.

1 Use the pointers to find the Pole Star. Sketch the Plough as you see it one night.

2 If you look carefully, you will see that one of the seven stars is, in fact, a double star. Which one is it?

3 Now, find Casseopeia and draw it (figure 5).

4 Make a sketch to show the position of the Plough, the Pole Star and Casseopeia carefully. The Milky Way runs through Casseopeia. There are lots of stars to be seen.

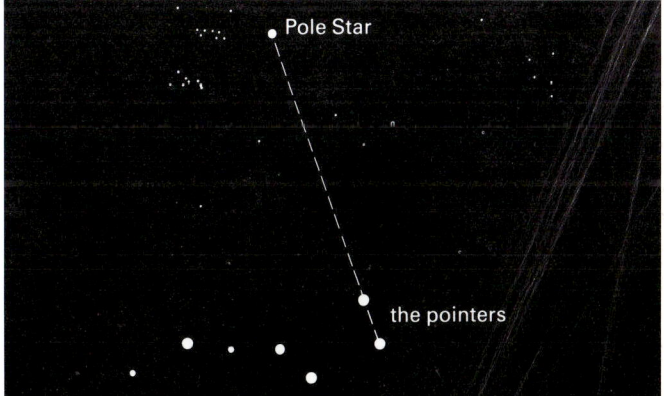

Figure 4

Figure 5

12 Black holes and supernovas

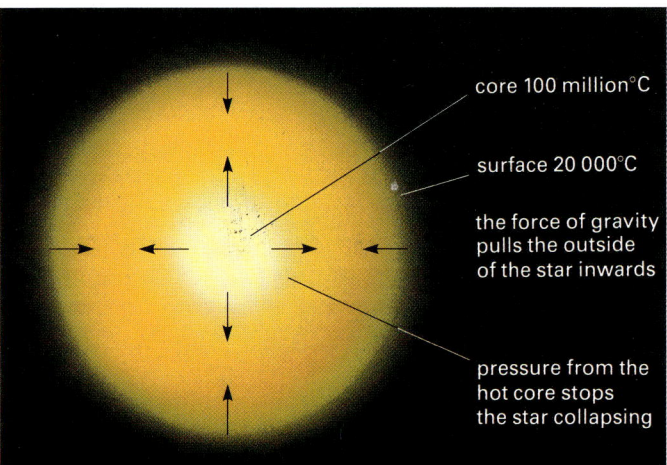

Figure 1

The Crab Nebula. In 1054, a bright new star was seen in the sky. We now think it was a supernova. This photo shows what the star looks like nearly 1000 years later

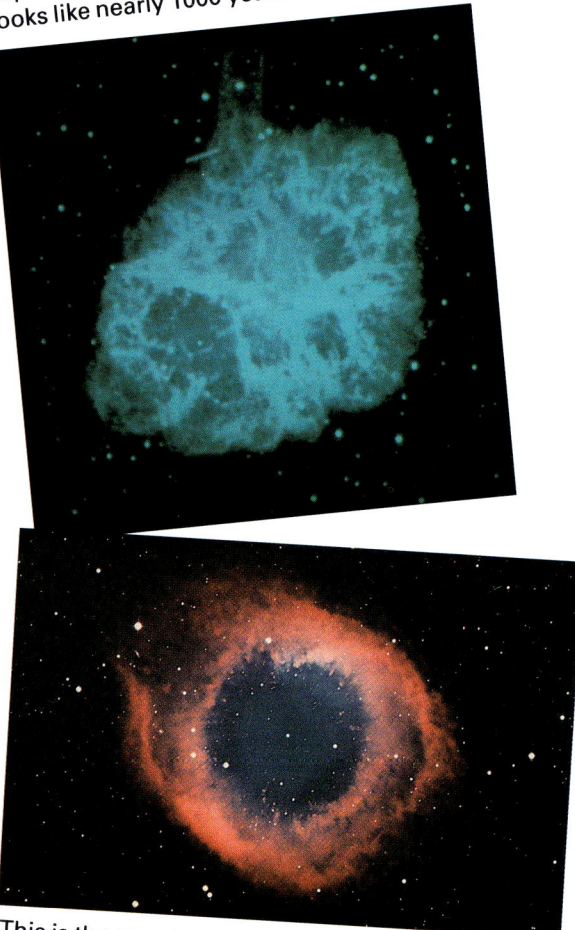

This is the remains of a nova. This star also shone brightly thousands of years ago

core 100 million°C

surface 20 000°C

the force of gravity pulls the outside of the star inwards

pressure from the hot core stops the star collapsing

Read the article below and then answer these questions on it. Look at figure 1 to help you.

For most of a star's life, it is very well behaved. It produces a lot of heat and light by a process known as **nuclear fusion**. Inside the star there is a fierce battle going on between two forces. The force of gravity pulls all parts of the star inwards. This force acts to make the star collapse. But the core where fusion occurs is very hot. The temperature in the core is 100 million °C in a large star. This makes a very large pressure which stops the star collapsing. The star burns constantly as long as these forces balance.

At the end of a star's life expectancy, things start to happen. If the fusion process gets too fast, the star blows up. These explosions are called **novas** or **supernovas**. Nova means 'new', so a nova is a new star. The reason these stars are called novas is that astronomers suddenly notice a new, bright star. In fact, the star is old and is dying, but it shines brightly and we notice it. A very large star, like a blue giant, can turn into a supernova. In this case the star destroys itself in a gigantic explosion. A supernova is so bright that it emits more light than an entire galaxy.

Most stars collapse at the end of their lives. Nuclear fusion in the core stops and there is nothing to stop the star collapsing. Our sun will collapse into a white dwarf. The diameter of the Sun will only be about the same size as the Earth's now. Some stars collapse so quickly that they turn into **black holes**. The pull of gravity is very strong in a black hole. The whole star is

squashed into a volume smaller than a pinhead. Nothing can escape its pull. Strange things happen near black holes. According to Einstein's theory of relativity, time slows down near a black hole. If you fall into one, it would seem to take an age to reach it. But somebody watching you would think you fell quickly.

1 What force acts to make stars collapse?
2 What is the core of a star?
3 What is a supernova?
4 Which is bigger, a white dwarf or a black hole?
5 How is a black hole made?
6 Sirius is 10 light years away from us. Imagine Sirius turned into a supernova. Explain what would happen to us.
7 Imagine you are aboard the Starship Enterprise as it falls into a blackhole. Could you escape? What would it be like? How long would it take to escape?

13 Winter constellations

This is an activity for a clear evening in January. A good time for it would be about 7 pm or 8 pm.

Go outside and look south. Find the bright constellation Orion (figure 2). Above Orion and to the right, you should see the star clusters of the Hyades and the Pleiades. Below Orion and to the left you will see Sirius.

1 What colour is Betelgeuse?
2 What colour is Aldebaran?
3 What colour is Rigel?
4 Which is the brightest star you can see?
5 Where is Orion's belt?
6 Where is Orion's sword? Look carefully at Orion's sword. Can you see a fuzzy area? This is the Orion **nebula**. It is a large cloud of hydrogen gas. The cloud is collapsing and new stars are being born in it. Look at the photo on the contents page.
7 If you have a pair of binoculars, look carefully at the Pleiades, Hyades and Orion's sword. Draw what you see.

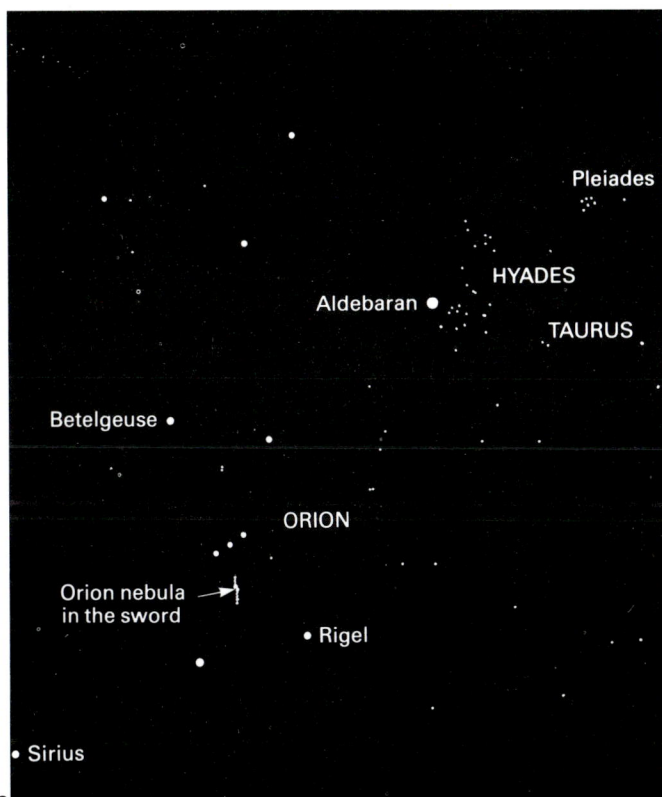

Figure 2

14 Finding Venus

Sometimes Venus appears in the evening and sometimes in the morning. When it appears in the evening, it is the first thing you see as the sun sets (figure 3).

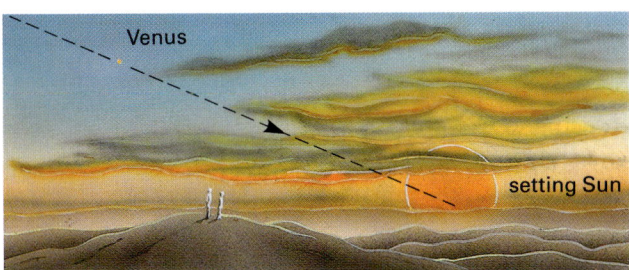

Figure 3

When Venus appears in the morning, you can still see it after all the other stars have vanished. Venus is the brightest heavenly body after the Sun and Moon. This is because it is so close to us.

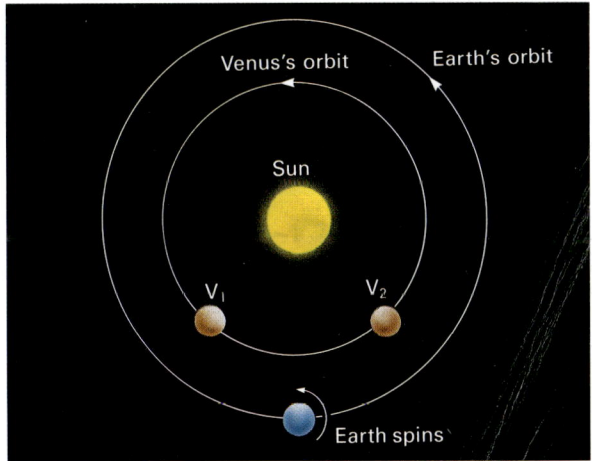

Figure 4

Look at the diagram above.

1 Explain why you always see Venus just after sunset or just before dawn.
2 In which position V_1 or V_2 do you see Venus in the morning?
3 Draw a diagram to show how you could find Venus in the morning.

27

15 Apollo 11

Study the series of photographs below. These are photographs of the *Apollo 11* mission to the moon. *Apollo 11* went to the Moon in July, 1969. Neil Armstrong and Buzz Aldrin were the first men to walk on the Moon.

1 Early in the morning of July 16th, the giant *Saturn* V rocket blasts off. The five F1 engines provide a thrust of 33 million newtons. The rocket accelerates upwards very quickly. This upwards acceleration makes the astronauts feel very heavy. At one point they feel 3 times as heavy as their normal weight. After going round the Earth, rockets speed *Apollo 11* towards the Moon

2 The astronauts are now on their way to the Moon. Here they hardly feel any weight at all. They are a long way from the Earth and Moon. Gravity only pulls them weakly. This is called zero-g

3 After a journey of nearly 4 days, the astronauts are in orbit round the Moon

4 The lunar module sets off for the Moon. The Earth looks very small – it is 400 000 km away

5 Neil Armstrong and Ed Aldrin set foot on the Moon. They gather samples of Moon rock to take back to Earth. Scientific equipment is left behind to gather information

6 The Earth appears large again as the astronauts approach home

7 After re-entering the Earth's atmosphere, the astronauts splash down into the Pacific Ocean. The helicopter approaches to pick them up

Now answer these questions about the *Apollo 11* mission.

1 Describe what the astronauts felt like during take off.
2 What problems do you think the astronauts had in zero-g? How do you think they managed to eat?
3 What dangers did the astronauts face when landing on the Moon? What would have happened if the ground had been soft? What would have happened if a space suit leaked?
4 Why did the astronauts have weighted boots? What was it like walking on the Moon?
5 Why can you see only half the Earth in the fourth photograph?

6 Re-entering the Earth's atmosphere was very dangerous. They had to come in at exactly the right angle. What would have happened if their angle was (i) too sharp? (ii) too shallow?
7 How was information sent back to Earth from the equipment left behind?
8 Every time a *Saturn V* rocket was launched it cost everybody in the USA one dollar. Was it a good way to spend money? Should Britain land a man or woman on the Moon?

16 Astronomy word quiz

Make a copy of the grid in figure 1. Answer the clues to find the missing astronomer.

1 This is a bright old star, not a new one!
2 He was the first astronomer to use a telescope.
3 You will never get out of this.
4 His comet only comes round every 76 years.
5 Mars has two of these.
6 Astronomers find this useful for seeing stars.
7 Andromeda is one of these.
8 A black mark on the Sun?
9 A pair of these makes things seem bigger.
10 Muddled ore met, streaks across the sky.
11 The biggest planet.
12 A group of stars near Orion.
13 This keeps your feet on the ground.
14 This planet shows phases.
15 This moon goes round Jupiter.
16 You will see these on the Moon.
17 The seventh planet.
18 The Sun is the centre of this.

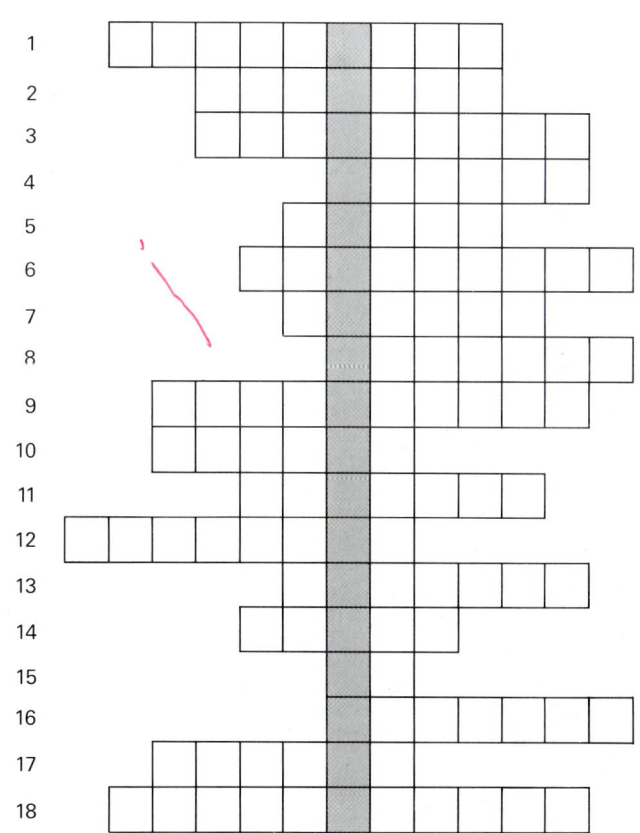

Figure 1

17 Comets, meteors, asteroids

Read the article. Then answer the questions that follow.

It is not just planets that go round the Sun. There are millions of small pieces of rocks that fly round the Sun in strange orbits. Most of these rocks are 4500 million years old. They are left over from the time when the solar system was formed. We think the solar system was made from an enormous ball of gas and rocks. The Sun and larger planets were formed from the gas. The Earth and other inner planets were made from the rock. But a lot of rocks were left over. Where are they now?

There are a lot of chunks of rock in orbit between Mars and Jupiter. These are called asteroids or planetoids. They are a lot of very small planets. The largest is called Ceres. It is 700 km in diameter.

Some lumps of rock and ice move round the Sun in strange or eccentric orbits. These are **comets**. The best

known is Halley's Comet. This returns every 76 years. We only see it when it is close to us. For most of the time it lies beyond Jupiter's orbit. The Sun produces a stream of particles, called the solar wind. This blows away bits of ice from the comet. This produces the comet's tail.

The Earth also passes through small streams of particles that move in orbits like comets. We call these small particles **meteors**. When we pass through these streams we see many bright streaks of light in the sky. These streaks occur when a meteor burns itself up in the atmosphere. These are sometimes called shooting stars. Very rarely a meteor is so big that it reaches the ground. Look at the photograph of the crater in the Arizona desert. This was caused by a meteor weighing several tons. It is thought the crater was made over 20 000 years ago.

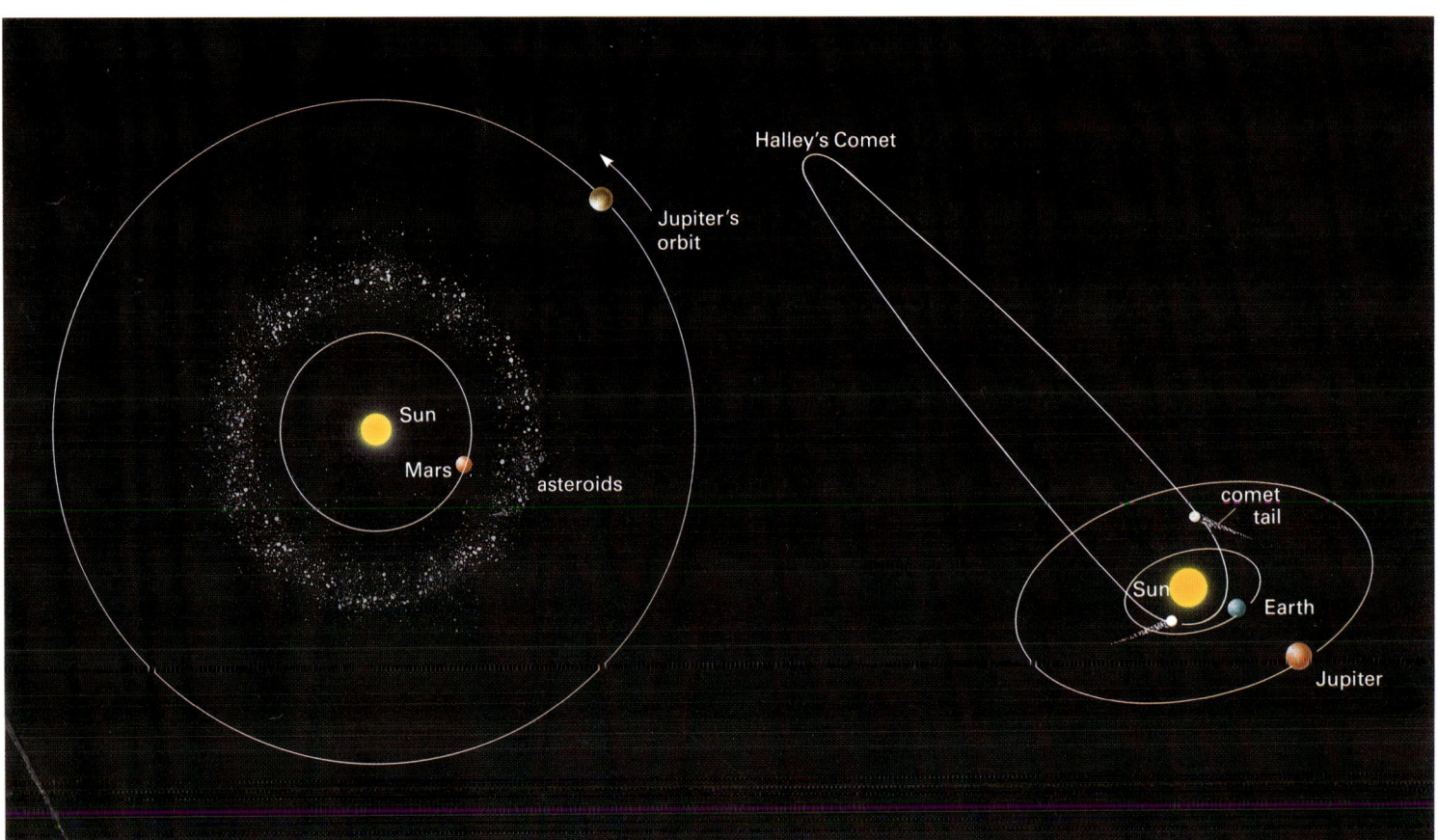

Figure 1

A comet

This photo was taken using a special sort of photography where the shutter is kept open for a longer period of time. The coloured arcs are star trails and the straight, horizontal line near the bottom is a meteor streak

A crater made by a fallen meteor in the Arizona desert

1 What is Ceres? How big is it?

2 What is a comet?

3 How long does Halley's comet take to go round the Sun?

4 Why do comets have tails? Why does the tail always point away from the Sun?

5 What is a meteor?

6 How are craters made?

7 Why do we see many craters on the Moon, but very few on the Earth?

8 Why are craters not formed on the Moon now? When were craters made?

18   Talking about space

Your teacher will divide the class up into groups of 2 or 3. Each group must prepare a 5 minute talk on a topic. You will find some facts in this book. You will need to go to the school library to find out some more. You should make some posters to help illustrate your talk.

Choose from one of these subjects:

■ the inner planets – Mercury and Venus

■ Mars

■ Jupiter and its moons

■ Saturn and its rings

■ the outer planets – Uranus, Neptune and Pluto

■ comets

■ the Sun

■ stars – from super giants to dwarfs

■ galaxies

■ landing on the Moon

■ the *Voyager* probe.

19   Word search

In this word search there are 20 objects you can find in the solar system. The answers can be written vertically, horizontally or diagonally, forwards or backwards.

1 These are useful for communications.
2 You'll find one on the Moon.
3 These are trenches on the Moon.
4 Uranus has 9 of these.
5 This goes round Uranus every 4 days.
6 An enormous moon.
7 A volcano on Mars.
8 Arms around a planet?
9 Outer most Galilean moon.
10 Lots between Mars and Jupiter.

11 Pluto's companion in the underworld.
12 The Sun is one of these.
13 This goes round the Sun 4 times a year.
14 We are the third. . . . .
15 The hottest planet.
16 Venus has clouds of this.
17 This went on a long journey.
18 These craft went to the Moon.
19 These have tails.
20 System centre.

S	B	X	K	D	O	L	L	O	P	A	Z	J	C	X	A
U	A	B	G	E	Y	R	U	C	R	E	M	V	A	P	O
L	C	T	H	W	A	T	Z	H	F	X	Y	U	L	R	L
P	J	Q	E	O	Z	B	I	Y	S	R	A	M	L	B	Y
H	Y	V	I	L	T	A	S	L	G	O	S	N	I	M	M
U	Q	E	U	S	L	T	L	G	N	P	T	K	S	W	P
R	R	P	L	U	R	I	E	F	I	Q	E	Q	T	P	U
I	N	W	K	L	R	E	T	A	R	C	R	J	O	V	S
C	S	C	F	V	O	I	G	E	F	S	O	G	Y	C	M
A	L	M	H	V	T	W	R	A	S	D	I	U	N	X	O
C	G	X	W	A	E	Q	D	Q	Y	L	D	U	I	T	N
I	U	L	N	L	R	K	S	W	P	O	S	D	N	E	S
D	T	S	E	M	O	C	U	A	R	V	O	K	N	Y	
H	J	F	C	T	J	O	N	M	N	R	N	H	L	A	I
R	U	M	B	R	I	E	L	E	M	E	F	G	C	L	Z
D	I	S	E	M	A	C	N	A	H	O	V	B	W	P	D

Figure 1